A Cat's Little
Instruction Book

Also available from Thorsons

Life's Little Instruction Book
Life's Little Instruction Book, Volume II
by H. Jackson Brown Jr

A Dog's Little Instruction Book
by David Brawn

A Cat's Little Instruction Book

Leigh W. Rutledge

HarperCollins*Publishers*

HarperCollins*Publishers*
77–85 Fulham Palace Road,
Hammersmith, London W6 8JB

www.**fire**and**water**.com

First published in the USA by Dutton, NAL, Penguin Books USA
Published in the UK by Thorsons 1993
Published by HarperCollins*Publishers* 1999

1 3 5 7 9 10 8 6 4 2

Illustrations by Mike Gordon

A catalogue record for this book
is available from the British Library

ISBN 0 7225 3909 6

Printed and bound in Great Britain by
Woolnough Bookbinding Ltd, Irthlingborough, Northants

To Beardsley, Spitfire
and Dr Tom Bird

- Always lick after meals

- When in doubt, chase something

- Keep your tail away from stoves, candles, lit cigarettes, automatic dishwasher doors, children, rocking-chairs and dogs. God only gave you one tail – take good care of it

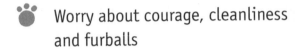 Worry about courage, cleanliness and furballs

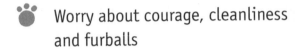 *Don't* worry about what other cats think of you. Remember, the cats who often do the most with their lives are the ones who were laughed at, ridiculed or made fun of as kittens

- Be adorable

- Stay out of car engines

- Stay out of open windows during thunderstorms

- Stay indoors on Bonfire Night

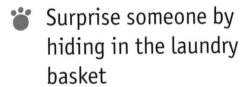 Surprise someone by hiding in the laundry basket

Avoid the temptation to spend all day waiting expectantly by the birdbath

Christmas trees are meant to be climbed

Long naps never go out of fashion

Just say no to catnip

The three Great Lies of Life are:

1 The cheque is in the post
2 All I want is one kiss
3 It'll be all right, just get in the travelling basket

- Avoid cleaning your private parts in public places

- Forgive your enemies – but hit them a couple of times first

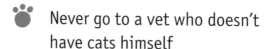 Never go to a vet who doesn't have cats himself

Never go back to a vet who discusses his or her stock portfolio while taking your temperature

Always make sure the lid is down on the toilet before jumping on it

Don't run to the vet's for every little ache and pain. Ninety percent of your medical problems will get better on their own, regardless of what you take or do for them

 Remember, no matter how much they love you, all human beings are biased towards their own species

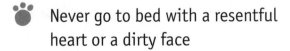 Never go to bed with a resentful heart or a dirty face

Learn to recognise the sound of a bowl being filled with cereal; milk usually follows

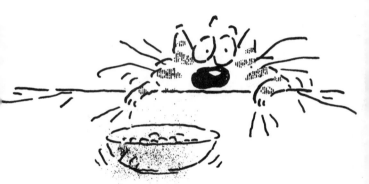

Be astonishingly
mysterious

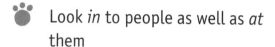 Look *in* to people as well as *at* them

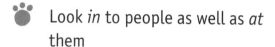 When depressed or confused, try lying on your back with your legs in the air; sometimes the world just looks better upside-down

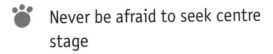 Never be afraid to seek centre stage

No matter what you've done wrong, always try to make it look like the dog did it

Sniff every stranger

 Never take a nap in a parked car –
you may wake up and find yourself
being carried off to a faraway
place

Don't eat anti-freeze, tinsel, broken Christmas-tree ornaments, straight pins, paper clips, strange pills lying on the bathroom floor, polystyrene or mice you suspect have just eaten rat poison

Cuddle someone you love on snowy afternoons

Sleep in a flowerbed to stay cool on hot summer days

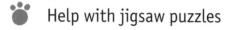 Help with jigsaw puzzles

 Avoid like the plague any person who has, within the last 12 months, picked you up and shaken you adoringly

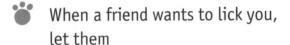 When a friend wants to lick you, let them

Never brood about the past. If you're ever tempted to, take a good hard look at the humans around you. They do it all the time – are *they* happy?

Forgive people who babble baby-talk in your face. They're only repeating what someone else taught them

 Learn the difference between idleness and repose – one wastes time, the other luxuriates in it

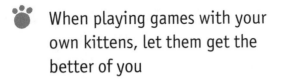 When playing games with your own kittens, let them get the better of you

When playing games with someone else's kittens, beat them up

Be a friend to people who have suffered grief, rejection, abuse, financial loss or recent illness. In moments of personal tragedy, human beings tend to run away from one another – learn from their bad example

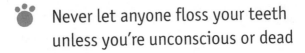 Never let anyone floss your teeth unless you're unconscious or dead

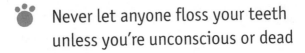 Let sleeping dogs lie – literally

Avoid vacuum cleaners

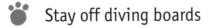 Stay off diving boards

Get your booster shots every year

- Take time to savour the view from every window in your house

- Never chew on electrical cords or wires

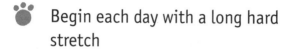 Begin each day with a long hard stretch

Never sleep too close to a fireplace that has a fire going in it

Remember that foxes, skunks and owls usually have the last word in any confrontation

Leave every dog with the impression that you are a lion cub who will be back to get even when you grow up

Never eat raw meat or stale leftovers. Always ask yourself: if it isn't something humans would feed their kids, why are they feeding it to *you*?

It's only an old wives' tale that a little litter tossed out of the cat box wards off the Devil. Make an effort to keep the area around your cat box clean

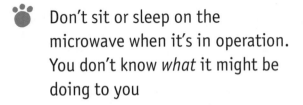 Don't sit or sleep on the microwave when it's in operation. You don't know *what* it might be doing to you

Watch out for human feet. (They won't watch out for you)

- Don't bite your nails

- Choose your loyalties carefully,
  but once you've chosen them put
  your heart and soul into them

Always clean between
your toes

Ignore any and all silly
propaganda about cats being
aloof, amoral, sinister, stupid
and false-hearted. The people
who believe such things are
themselves more often than not
aloof, amoral, sinister, stupid
and false-hearted

Run away and hide the moment you hear any group of human beings speculating about whether cats always land on their feet

 Become a force to be reckoned with – but don't run it into the ground

Stay out of the rain

Stay out of the snow

Stay out of the tumble dryer

Seek out good hiding places

 Look both ways before crossing the street. Never *dart*. Better yet, don't cross streets

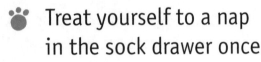 Treat yourself to a nap
in the sock drawer once
in a while

When climbing trees, never be satisfied with the lowest limb. However, bear in mind that most firemen have better things to do than get cats out of trees. If you get stuck, you're pretty much on your own

Avoid packs of roving children.
A child alone can sometimes be
dealt with, but once in a herd
they often turn into berserk
little creatures trying to impress
one another

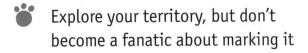 Explore your territory, but don't become a fanatic about marking it

Roll in the dirt at least once a week to maintain a healthy and beautiful coat

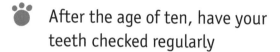 After the age of ten, have your teeth checked regularly

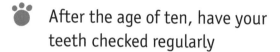 Learn the difference between a pair of shoes and a litter box

Never worry about vet's or cat food bills. Someone else will pay them

 Don't be fooled by cat furniture – tiny beds, cramped baskets, etc. – sold in pet shops. Human furniture is always more plush and comfortable

🐾 Let your emotions get the best of you sometimes

🐾 Cultivate bedroom eyes when asking for things. If you're ignored, don't be afraid to put a little bit of claw into your request

- Climb the living room curtains to develop upper-body strength

- Resist an urge to leap onto the ceiling fan, especially when it's in motion

Own nothing, and be owned by no one

Chase and bite human toes through the bedcovers

Remember that every baby
bird you encounter has
a mother who would be
heartbroken if you ate it

Never be discouraged by the words, No, Stop that, or Bad Cat

 Never be overly concerned when someone screams, If you ever do that again, I'm going to make you live outside! It's almost always an idle threat

To make a lasting impression at parties, sit in the onion dip or stick your head in the punchbowl and start slurping loudly. If all else fails, perch yourself like a vulture on the arm of a sofa and leave all the guests with the impression that if they don't finish the hors d'oeuvres soon, *you* will

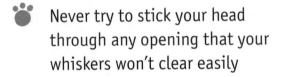 Never try to stick your head through any opening that your whiskers won't clear easily

Ignore any endeavour whose primary goal is self-improvement.

🐾 Don't worry about little things

🐾 Don't worry about big things

🐾 Surprise the entire household by unrolling all the toilet paper at night

 Never purr half-heartedly

 Never yawn half-heartedly

Never eat more than your own weight in table scraps

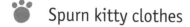 Spurn kitty clothes

Never let anyone dye your hair a funny colour or give you a trendy haircut

Eschew coloured bows or plastic barettes

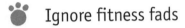 Ignore fitness fads

Say Yes! to armchairs, cut flowers, stomach tickling and tuna fish

Inspire whimsy in everyone you meet

- Remember – meow and the world meows with you; hiss and you hiss alone

- Force people to throw you off their laps at least three times before conceding that they actually mean it

- Take time to sit on the grass and watch the clouds roll by

- Chase butterflies

- No matter how old you are, never be afraid to express the kitten within

Don't play in plastic bags

Keep in mind that just because a man or woman is poor or even homeless it doesn't mean they can't be a loving and devoted companion. There is absolutely *no* correlation between money and a good heart

Refuse to retrieve things

 Protest loudly if anyone ever
suggests getting a new puppy

Keep everybody's secrets

Ignore your mistakes

Scratch your ears regularly

Pose for photos

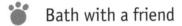 Bath with a friend

 Learn to watch everything, even with your eyes closed

Never join anything

 Persuade people to devote their free time to petting you

Steer clear of wasps, bees, ants
and spiders. At best, they make
iffy playmates; at worst, they're
hazardous between meal-snacks

The three best rainy day activities are:

1 Sleeping

2 Napping

3 Taking it easy

The three best late night activities are:

1 Chasing a ping-pong ball around the bathtub

2 Dragging underwear, tights and socks from room to room

3 Climbing and hanging from the blinds while wailing loudly

Be suspicious of anyone whose clothes are immaculate and completely free of cat hairs. It means they either don't like cats or don't hug the ones they have

Be inscrutable

 Be regal

 Be nobody's fool

- Don't waste time watching television

- Don't waste time staring in mirrors

- Don't waste time trying to figure out the meaning of life

Don't introduce yourself to new neighbours by sharpening your claws on their patio furniture or playing in their flowerbeds. First impressions can rarely be undone

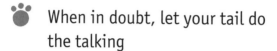 When in doubt, let your tail do the talking

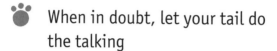 Drink lots of water

 Play and sleep in cardboard boxes

Resist any impulse to fall asleep in your food dish

For mild stomach upsets, eat plenty of grass. If that fails, try a little yoghurt

 Make friends with the milkman

Help with making the bed

Help with re-decorating, even if no one asks you

Help with making dinner

To stay warm on cold winter days, sleep on the sill of an east window in the morning and a west window in the afternoon. That way, you'll catch the sunshine

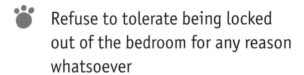 Refuse to tolerate being locked out of the bedroom for any reason whatsoever

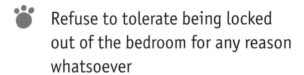 Moult a lot

Control your temper

 Avoid acting on jealous impulses,
no matter how justified they seem
at the time

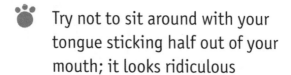

Try not to sit around with your tongue sticking half out of your mouth; it looks ridiculous

Beware of guns

- Avoid second-hand cigarette smoke

- When kneading someone's stomach, stop just short of drawing blood

Push your luck

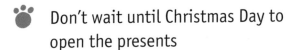 Don't wait until Christmas Day to open the presents

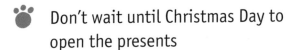 Don't whine when your toys disappear under the refrigerator or down the heating ducts. Accept the fact that life can be brutally unfair at times

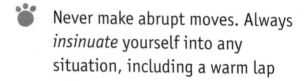 Never make abrupt moves. Always *insinuate* yourself into any situation, including a warm lap

Regard all neatly stacked piles of paper as provocation

🐾 Don't just inhabit a house;
become its *soul*

🐾 Learn to develop a memorable
meow

🐾 Find any excuse to run up and
down the stairs dementedly

- Retain your sense of wonder about all things

- Retain your curiosity

- Refrain from giving anyone a dead mouse or bird as a present; your idea of the perfect gift may not be somebody else's

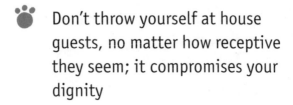

Don't throw yourself at house guests, no matter how receptive they seem; it compromises your dignity

Steer clear of cacti

Never eat pork

● Never run across a recently mopped floor; you could slip and hurt yourself

● Don't cry over spilt milk — lap it up instead

● Bestow love bites sparingly and only to those who will understand the spirit in which they were meant

Always look astonished when you break something, even if you meant to do it

Always sleep under the covers. Humans will never throw you out if you snuggle under the covers with them

Stay out of rubbish bins and skips unless you or someone you love is starving

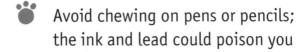 Avoid chewing on pens or pencils;
the ink and lead could poison you

Resist the temptation to claw
strangers who make dense remarks
like 'Isn't it amazing? Every cat
almost has its own personality'

If you ever find yourself homeless, remember: look pathetic, not sickly. You want to inspire sympathy, not visions of vet's bills. And don't forget to purr disarmingly

 Lay claim to every jacket, sweater and shirt as soon as it lands on a chair

Don't waste time learning to do things that others will do for you

When a child starts screaming or crying loudly, resist the temptation to sit on its face

Become a paragon of sanity, sensuality and contentment

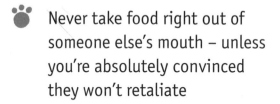 Never take food right out of someone else's mouth – unless you're absolutely convinced they won't retaliate

Never retract your claws completely, except with your very best friends

Never bite the hand that feeds you – except as a last resort

- Never try to be something you're not

- Never give in to vulgarity

- Never be too smart for your own good

🐾 Trust your intuition

🐾 Tread silently

🐾 Knock small things off counters

Avoid shoving your private parts in people's faces, no matter how well you think you know them

Always enter a room with poise and confidence. If you accidentally slip or stumble, stop immediately. Start licking yourself rigorously – it distracts would-be hecklers

 Learn to recognize the difference between ordinary cans being opened and cat food cans being opened

- Chase all shoelaces

- If someone breaks into the house when no one else is there, hide. Leave the heroics to dogs

- Remember: everyone likes to wake up to a kiss

Sleep under table lamps

Sleep on the answering machine

Sleep in the middle of the hall

Be bold

Be winsome

Be wildly tender

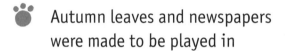 Autumn leaves and newspapers were made to be played in

Sleeping in the sunlight is often the best medicine for whatever ails you

Make the world your scratching post

Never sleep alone

Become someone's friend for life